WEIRD AND UNUSUAL ANIMALS

FRILLED LIZARDS

by Allan Morey

AMICUS HIGH INTEREST • AMICUS INK

Amicus High Interest and Amicus Ink are imprints of Amicus
P.O. Box 1329, Mankato, MN 56002
www.amicuspublishing.us

Library of Congress Cataloging-in-Publication Data
Names: Morey, Allan, author.
Title: Frilled lizards / by Allan Morey.
Description: Mankato, Minnesota : Amicus, 2017. | Series: Weird and
  unusual animals | Includes index. | Audience: Grades K to 3.
Identifiers: LCCN 2016042396 (print) | LCCN 2016054513 (ebook) | ISBN
  9781681511573 (library binding) | ISBN 9781681521886 (pbk.) | ISBN
  9781681512471 (ebook)
Subjects: LCSH: Frilled lizard--Juvenile literature.
Classification: LCC QL666.L223 M67 2017 (print) | LCC QL666.L223
(ebook) | DDC 597/.61--dc23
LC record available at https://lccn.loc.gov/2016042396

Photo Credits: tets/Shutterstock background pattern; Belinda Wright/
Getty cover photograph; Eric Isselée/iStock 2, 22; Dave Watts/Alamy
Stock Photo 4-5; Andrew Watson/Alamy Stock Photo 7; Robert Valentic/
NPL/Minden Pictures 8-9; FLPA/Gianpiero Ferrari/AgeFotoStock 10-11;
Mary Evans Picture Library Ltd/AgeFotoStock 12-13; Genevieve Vallee/
Alamy Stock Photo 15; blickwinkel/Alamy Stock Photo 16-17; jeridu/
iStock 18-19; adogslifephoto/iStock 20-21

Editor: Wendy Dieker
Designer: Aubrey Harper
Photo Researcher: Holly Young

Printed in the United States of America

HC 10 9 8 7 6 5 4 3 2 1
PB 10 9 8 7 6 5 4 3 2 1

TABLE OF CONTENTS

SCARY LIZARDS

Most of the time, frilled lizards look like other lizards. They have long tails. **Scales** cover their bodies. But when danger is near, look out! A scary **frill** pops up.

LOOKING BIG

The frill usually lies across the lizard's neck. Muscles in its jaws connect to the frill. To look big, the lizard opens its mouth wide. This opens the frill.

Weird but True
Frilled lizards also **hiss** loudly. This scares enemies, too.

WARM HOME

Most frilled lizards live in **woodlands** in northern Australia. It is a warm place with lots of trees. Some can be found on Papua New Guinea. This island is near Australia.

PREDATORS

Frilled lizards grow up to 3 feet (1 m) long. But big **predators** are around. Snakes try to eat frilled lizards. Large birds chase them. Big cats and **dingoes** hunt them. Most of the time, frilled lizards get away.

Weird but True
The frill actually works! Not many frilled lizards get eaten by predators.

RUNNING AWAY

Sometimes looking big doesn't scare away a predator. The frilled lizard has another trick. It runs away to hide. It zigzags off to the trees. Zoom!

UP IN THE TREES

Frilled lizards have sharp claws. They also have long tails. These help them climb trees. Their coloring makes them look like tree branches. Trees are good hiding places for these lizards.

HUNTERS

Frilled lizards eat some plants. But they mostly eat small animals. They catch bugs and spiders. They feed on mice. They hunt small lizards and snakes.

YOUNG LIZARDS

Frilled lizards **mate** in fall. Females then dig nests. They lay about 25 eggs underground. Eggs **hatch** in about three months. Young lizards take care of themselves.

Weird but True
Baby lizards are born with a frill. They know how to use it right away!

LITTLE DRAGONS

Frilled lizards can look like something out of a fairy tale. They sort of look like a dragon. Some people do call them frilled dragons. That scary name fits!

A LOOK AT FRILLED LIZARDS

WORDS TO KNOW

dingo – a dog-like animal that lives in Australia

frill – something extra, like an extra piece of skin

hatch – to break out of an egg

hiss – to make a sharp sound like the letter *s*

mate – to pair up to produce young

predator – an animal that hunts other animals for food

scale – a small, flat piece of skin that covers a reptile's body

woodlands – areas of land with many trees and shrubs

LEARN MORE

Books

Marsh, Laura. *Lizards*. Washington, D.C.: National Geographic Society, 2012.

Spilsbury, Louise. *Superstar Reptiles*. New York: PowerKids Press, 2015.

Websites

National Geographic—Frilled Lizards
http://animals.nationalgeographic.com/animals/reptiles/frilled-lizard

San Diego Zoo—Lizards
http://animals.sandiegozoo.org/animals/lizard

INDEX